THE POET SLAVE
OF CUBA

A BIOGRAPHY OF
JUAN FRANCISCO MANZANO

MARGARITA ENGLE
ART BY SEAN QUALLS

SQUARE
FISH
HENRY HOLT AND COMPANY
NEW YORK

SQUARE
FISH

An Imprint of Macmillan

THE POET SLAVE OF CUBA. Text copyright © 2006 by Margarita Engle. Illustrations
copyright © 2006 by Sean Qualls. All rights reserved. Printed in the United States of America
by LSC Communications, Harrisonburg, Virginia. For information, address Square Fish,
175 Fifth Avenue, New York, NY 10010.

Library of Congress Cataloging-in-Publication Data
Engle, Margarita.
The poet slave of Cuba: a biography of Juan Francisco Manzano / Margarita Engle ;
illustrations by Sean Qualls.
p.   cm.
ISBN 978-0-312-65928-8
1. Manzano, Juan Francisco, 1797–1854—Juvenile poetry. 2. Children's poetry,
American. 3. Slaves—Juvenile poetry. 4. Poets—Juvenile poetry. 5. Cuba—Juvenile
poetry. I. Qualls, Sean. II. Title.
PS3555.N4254 P64 2006   811'.54—dc22   2005046200

Originally published in the United States by Henry Holt and Company
First Square Fish Edition: March 2011
Square Fish logo designed by Filomena Tuosto
Book designed by Patrick Collins
mackids.com

10 9

AR: 6.3 / LEXILE: NP

This book is dedicated to censored poets everywhere and to my hundreds of cousins in Cuba.
—M. E.

To my loving mother
—S. Q.

Te sigan los cantares
De la paz, del amor, y buen destino
Que ofrece al Bardo que sus linfas besa
Virtud, inspiración, y fortaleza.

Songs follow you
Of peace, love, and good fortune
Offered to the poet who kisses these waters
Virtue, inspiration, and strength.

FROM "A LA LUNA" ("TO THE MOON")
BY JUAN FRANCISCO MANZANO
THE POET SLAVE OF CUBA
1797–1853

THe POeT SLAVe OF CUBA

JUAN

My mind is a brush made of feathers
    painting pictures of words
    I remember
    all that I see
    every syllable
    each word a twin of itself
    telling two stories
    at the same time
    one of sorrow
    the other hope

I love the words
    written with my feathery mind
    in the air
    and with my sharp fingernails
    on leaves in the garden

When my owner catches
    a whiff
    of the fragrance
    of words
    engraved in the flesh
    of succulent geranium leaves
    or the perfumed petals of *alelí* flowers

then she frowns because she knows
that I dream
with my feathers
my wings

Poetry cools me, syllables calm me
I read the verses of others
the free men
and know
that I'm never alone

Poetry sets me aflame
I grow furious
dangerous, a blaze
of soul and heart, a fiery tongue
a lantern at midnight

My first owner was sweet to me
I was her pet, a new kind of poodle
my pretty mother chosen
to be her personal handmaid

My mother
María del Pilar Manzano
a slave

Together we belonged
along with countless others

human beasts of burden
to Doña Beatriz de Jústiz, La Marquesa
the proud Marchioness Jústiz de Santa Ana
noble wife of Don Juan Manzano
who shares my name
even though
he is not
my father

Don Juan rules El Molino
   his plantation
   on this island of sugar
   and many other
   sweet illusions

These were my mother's duties:
   dress La Marquesa
   undress her
   cool her skin with a palm-leaf fan
   answer questions
   never ask
   collect milk from new mothers
   in the huts
   near the fields
   slave milk, the lotion used for softening
   the skin
   of noble ladies

This my mother accomplished:
  deliver the milk
  grind eggshells and rice into powder
  for making *la cascarilla*
  a pale shell for hiding
  the darkness
  of Spaniards
  who pretend
  to be pale
  in our presence

When the noble ladies go out in public
  milk-soothed, eggshell-crusted
  masked and disguised
  we no longer look the same
  dark owner
  and dark slaves

Now my owner is ghostly
  inside her skeleton of powder
  but I, being only a poodle,
  can watch
  I am allowed
  to know
  these truths
  about shadow
  and bright

So I listen
    when the ghost-owner calls me her own baby
    she plays with me
    and even decides
    to set my true mother
    free

Free to marry Toribio de Castro
    a man also promised
    his freedom

My father is winged, like my mother
    oh, I envy them
    what will happen
    to me
    little bird
    left behind in this haunted nest?

She takes me with her wherever she goes
I become the companion of my owner, noble ghost
    no, not a companion, remember?
    a poodle, her pet
    with my curly dark hair
    and small child's brown skin
    suitable
    for the theater
    and parties

So I bark
    on command
    I learn to whine and howl
    in verse
I'm known as the smart one who never
    forgets
I can listen
    then recite
    every word

Listen, she says to her friends
and the priest
    see how little Juanito can sing
    see how I've trained him
    watch him
    perform

Back and forth
    over and over
    country home, city home, palaces, the plantation
    only six years old, she says
    but listen to his big funny
    voice

Back and forth
    over and over
    I recite strange words in several languages
    Spanish, Latin, French

while my sweet ghost-Mamá-owner
and all her friends
listen
they are forgetful
I am rememberful
I remember there is also one more mother
in my song
a bird-mother
caged
but winged

MARÍA DEL PILAR

My son knows all the lines
   of every play he's seen performed
   he knows the lyrics of songs
   and the rhymes
   of sonnets and ballads
   he knows the Psalms I've taught him
   the sermons he's heard at church
   the prayers of strangers
   and curses too
   all the words of a world
   observed
   for six years

Everyone applauds at the parties
   they always giggle and clap
   so delighted
   the ladies wearing satin dresses
   embroidered with jewels and pearls
   seeing them, you'd think
   we're the clay
   of earth's daylight
   while they're distant nights
   filled with stars

Why isn't he frightened,
   so young, so observant?
Why doesn't he just play and pretend to forget
like the rest of us do
when we're watched?

JUAN

~ ~ ~ ~ ~

One mother can leave and be free
   but she won't
   not without me
The other one is angry with my father,
   Toribio,
   who sews and plays the harp
   my father
   who picked me up and shook me
   calling me spoiled
   like a prince

Can't he tell the difference between a prince
   and a poodle?

This is how the ghost-Mamá punishes my father:
   with silence
   her invisible
   whip
If the priest hadn't spoken to her, the silence
   might have gone on and on forever
   the silence
   I secretly
   treasured

Doña Beatriz

~ ~ ~ ~ ~

The boy is much cleaner than poodles and parrots
    or the Persian cats
    that are always shedding their fur on my pillows
    I treat him like my own
    I tell him he's the child of my old age
    I stroke his curly hair and hold him in my arms
Oh, how beautifully he behaves!
Not a rebel
    like his father, Toribio
Not a servant
    like his mother, María del Pilar
The boy is a genius
    a pleasure to behold
    a wonder to hear
I take him in my coach and he sits beside me
    calling me Mamá
    he barely knows his other mother anymore
    now I am the real one
    if only he weren't quite
    so dark

When I leave the country houses, city houses, palaces
    when I leave without him, oh, how he screams!
    Everyone laughs

he's inconsolable
how amusing, they say,
the child actually thinks he belongs to you—
in that other way
of belonging

JUAN

~~ ~~ ~~ ~~ ~~

What a find,
   the ladies exclaim,
   when I recite the *Iliad*, the *Odyssey*, the Catechism
   and long, dull foreign operas
   words that make no sense
   and long, boring sermons
   in Latin
   and silly plays
   that make everyone giggle
   behind the shields
   of their open silk fans

Ha, ha, a genius, isn't it entertaining
   ay, how precious
   what a find

The ghostly ladies masked and hidden
   inside their casings of eggshell-and-rice powder
   so no one can tell
   if they are dark too
   I watch
   as they arch their eyebrows
   and flutter their open silk fans

each fan the graceful shape
of a single wing
Even a free bird is helpless
with just one wing

DOÑA BEATRIZ

At his baptism I gave his mother such a wondrous,
    amazing gift
    everyone gasped
    Doña Beatriz is a saint, they said,
    not even waiting until she's
    on her deathbed
    to buy her way into heaven
    Imagine
    showing mercy so far ahead of time
    what a grand act of compassion!

The musicians were playing their harps and flutes
    the music of heaven
    his other mother's heart was drumming
    and his rebel father's eyes were roaring
    genius, I announced, the brilliant child
    of my old age

My proclamation was not trivial
    so I lifted my arms in a sweeping gesture
    my bosom grand,
    my fingers waving to show everyone
    the treasures I was free to give
    my houses were filled with such choices,

such gifts, so easily granted
all I had to do was choose one,
a painting or a marble statue
gold and silver coins
lampstands and jewels from Persia
furniture inlaid with ebony and cedar
from this island's dark, fragrant forests

I fingered the massive pendant at my neck
   diamonds, rubies, and emeralds
   all joined in a single design

Just one gift
   that was all I had to choose for a baptism
   One pearl or one coin would have been plenty
   one slim gold chain
   or carved toy

Instead, I made the announcement
   the one I had been keeping secret
   although I fear he must have guessed
   because he didn't look quite as pleased
   as I had imagined

So I wept, I dabbed my eyes with a lace kerchief
   I said the word, that one word
   they all wait for, so patiently and foolishly
   all their lives

Manumission!
I made it a big word
I waited, said it again
in its simpler forms
Freedom
Liberty
Libertad
all such fine words
so generous

My proclamation continued
in honor, I explained, of the baptism of this genius
the child of my old age
I give manumission to María del Pilar
for the price
of only three hundred pesos

And later, maybe Toribio as well
for only three hundred more pesos
and furthermore,
I hereby proclaim that from this day forward
I will abide by the Free Belly custom
of declaring all the future children
of María del Pilar and Toribio
free even long before birth, while still in the belly
hidden inside their mother
hidden, yet already free
even before she has earned and paid

her own three hundred pesos
the price of the court documents
she will someday carry
to keep the bounty hunters at bay
to keep them from seeing her and imagining
that she is a runaway headed for the mountains
ready to hide
ready to die

Ay, but my proclamation was so generous
that by the end everyone was weeping
even Juan, especially Juan
and strangely, also his mother and father
as if they imagined that three hundred pesos
could be considered
a fortune

Only Juanito, I said very clearly,
to make sure no one had misunderstood,
only this genius of my old age,
do I keep for myself
as my own
mine until the day of my death
when he will also
know mercy

María del Pilar

My son is not free, but I am, just as soon as . . .
   oh, but how does a prisoner like me
   find ways to earn and save such a fortune?
   How?

Imagine the shock, the excitement
   the anger, pure rage
Leave my son behind, how?
He is not hers, I won't let her have him
   why does she insist
   that he is the child of her old age?
Life is not logical, nothing makes sense
   how can this be, one child a slave
   —my child, my only child—
   while the others, unborn,
   are already proclaimed free?

I'll stay with you, Juanito, I promise
I'll always live close, in some hut of mud
   or shack of palm leaves
   your father and I, and all the rest, those still
     unborn
   your brothers and sisters of the future

we will not leave you behind
you will see us, we promise
But you must promise this
please vow that you will not listen
when she calls you the child of her old age
do not listen, do not believe her, and please
never pray
for her death
even though it is the only thing you will wish for
in secret
just as I,
without wanting to wish such a thing
in the presence of God,
already find my silent self
imagining

TORIBIO

~ ~ ~ ~ ~

She sends him away for a few hours each day
to the home of his godmother
to learn words

Imagine
    how he must feel in that other home
    where he learns the words
    of verses, plays, sermons, sonnets
    now he's a parrot, not a poodle
    he listens, listens, listens
    repeats every sound he hears
    from every book in his godmother's library

The applause
    when he recites at parties amazes him
    just as he amuses them with his French operas,
    a jumble of sound
    meaningless
    in my ears

They toss him gifts of coins and jewels
    silk kerchiefs

the plumes of rare birds
as if he could make wings of feathers and words
instead of playing with these toys
in his cage

JUAN

Three hundred pesos, is it a lot?
I like to imagine that I already have enough
    to buy them all
    mother, father, unborn brothers and sisters
    myself

Imagine
    what it would be like
    to buy yourself
    and wrap yourself up in a package
    and walk away
    carrying yourself
    under your arm
    like a book

Imagine
    how it will happen
    in just a few years
    on the day
    of her death
    doesn't she wonder
    how it feels to know that all I need now
    is a swift ending for her
    in order to make a sweet beginning for me?

María del Pilar

I hear him, I listen, he whispers
    things other children don't know how to know
    strange words about wings and dreams,
    cages
    feathers, freedom
    death

I see him staring with those eyes
    wondering
    making me wonder
    how soon she'll die
    a frightening thought
    because if it is soon
    and if I wish or, even worse, pray
    that it will happen
    then his freedom is granted
    only as her deathbed way of imagining
    that she can buy a ticket to enter heaven
    with that one good deed
    all will be meaningless for me
    if I lose
    my own good sense
    my kindness
    my God

The other day he recited words so completely new
    that I understood the verse
    was his own
    not borrowed, memorized,
    begged from the godmother's books

Soaring
    he said
Spirit
    he whispered
Imprisoned
    he murmured
    and then he went on

I only caught a few fragments
    of his rhyme of delight,
    something about a golden beak
    something about singing
    and wishes
    and hope

TORIBIO

Now they call my son the Golden Beak
and hearing such a flattering nickname, I ask
myself, I ask others, I even ask God:

Where is the rest of the bird?

JUAN

~ ~ ~ ~ ~

Here is the house I live in
    imagine, listen, look, see
    breathe in the fragrance of blossoms
    and fruit trees
    tall and green in the roofless central courtyard
    under that tiny square of sky
    visible from deep inside
    the heart of a place
    surrounded
    by stiffly walled rooms

Mangos, orchids, jasmine, lime
    these are the scents I inhale every morning
    when I step into the courtyard
    and look up at that small square of blue
    where birds in flight pass high above
    the rhythm of rising and falling wings
    daring me
    to scratch rhymes
    by pressing the sharpness of my fingernail
    into the soft flesh
    of petals and leaves
    even though I don't know
    how to write

Would they clap for me at those parties if they knew
    about the funny shapes I invent
    like a bird's sharp little feet scratching shapes
    on moist beach sand?

Would they clap if they knew that for me
    each secret shape is seen and remembered
    as my own private alphabet
    of make-believe letters
    and words?

María del Pilar

Three hundred pesos
   what a long time it takes
   for a mother to earn so much money
   to buy herself free
Only on Sunday afternoons do I have the choice
   of working for coins I can save
   here they are
   just a few
so I work and work while my son does his chores
   learning trades so that someday
   when she is dead and he is free
   what a fine tailor he will become
   like his father, my own Toribio, love of my life
   sewing fragments of linen and silk
   to hold the pieces of our lives in place
   with tight, careful stitches
   seams
   buttons, hooks
like the hook-shaped fingers of the men
   who work all day in the sun in the sugar fields
   grasping each tall cane with the left hand
   then chopping it down with the right hand
   holding a huge knife, *el machete*
   the long knife I pray my husband will never be

tempted to use
in an effort to speed the slow aging of our owner
as she moves
step by step
toward her natural
death.

JUAN

~ ~ ~ ~ ~

I am the big brother of two freeborn babies, twins
    a brother and sister, my own,
    free, so free,
    while I am not.

Eleven years old and now it has happened
    there she is
    on her deathbed
    arms crossed
    eyes closed
    ghostly mask of powdered eggshells and rice
    still in place
    hiding her darkness

No matter how much I scream, shriek, weep, pray
    she will not live again
    she who called me the child
    of her old age

Don't cry, my other mother, the real one, whispers
    this is the end
    of your sadness
    now you are free!

But I'm not
    it's a trick
    one swift trip

to the house
    of my godparents
    and then to La Marquesa
    instead of the long-promised
    freedom.

María del Pilar

~ ~ ~ ~ ~

Five years have passed,
    and I have not been allowed
    to see my son, not even once!
We heard whispers that somehow he'd learned
    to read.
Imagine!
    No, I cannot imagine five years without my son
    and yet, it's true
    the unimaginable.

Reading? Such a scandal, his fine gift
    of genius
    along with secret tutoring
    from someone I must leave nameless
    a man who dared to teach
    after hearing him in the courtyard
    inventing verses,
    trying to scratch them
    like birds' feet on sand
    into the soft flesh
    of leaves.

TORIBIO

Tricks
    always tricks
    free, not free
    this Marquesa de Prado Ameno
    his owner
    she is vile,
    they say she's a madwoman, crazy, cruel.

I only know this much:
    she makes him wear the clothes of a page
    blue satin jacket, scarlet pants
    trim of gold braid
    diamond pin
    black velvet hat
    with two red feathers.

At least his brother and sister are free
    the twins, our freeborn children
    the girl living
    the boy dead, but free and flying
    in heaven
    winged
    no need for a hat
    with red feathers.

JUAN

Even though I am not free
    there are things that I love
    in this world, this mansion, palace
    this strange home where I live
    even though it doesn't always feel exactly
    like living
    or home

I love to sit in the central courtyard
    looking up at a ceiling of sky
    looking around at the fragrant garden
    of jasmine and tuberose
    looking down at mosaics on the floor
    chips of tile swirled into stories
    of kings and castles
    jungles and beasts

I love the singing fountain, ripening fruit trees
    a view of high balconies dancing in wind
    the rhythm of archways and columns
    railings of wrought iron in the shapes
    of black metal peacocks
    and angels playing harps

I like to think that the angels are real
the music mine

I roam the vast rooms
filled with paintings and statues
I dance in the ballroom when no one is looking
I try out the musical instruments
I sit in the rocking chairs, swaying
to my own secret song
a silent moment
of peace

La Marquesa de Prado Ameno

~ ~ ~ ~ ~

One more small boy-slave
 crowded onto the
 between-place
 el entresol, the mezzanine
 where he can hear me when I call
 but he cannot see me
 by looking up
 even though I can see him
 by looking down.

Here I am
 tormented
 by one more annoying
 rascal
 always reciting
 his memorized poems
 always sneaking peeks
 at my books.

Every time I catch him reading
 under a table
 or behind a door

I lock him down in the cellar
with the charcoal
to darken his thoughts
and his skin.

Juan

This is the cellar,
imagine, the fear
no floorboards, no blanket, no food
even though it's only for one day
and one night
      or maybe a little more
      just enough time to let the whip do its job
imagine, no water,
      that's the worst,
and this silence
      except for my voice trapped inside my head
      whispering verses, rhymes, curses, songs, prayers
      strange, meaningless words
and some other voice too, a comforting one,
      maybe God's
but there's the stench too, that's the devil,
      this stink of rotting garbage
      and the dampness, foul rats and ghosts,
      all the evil enchantments
the screams of another voice, a hateful one.
No. Is it true? Can it be?
How is it possible?
Is this dreadfully shrieking voice really
      my own?

I would starve
    but there are boys around my age, more or less
The boys are her sons.
Don Nicolás is the merciful one
    a whispering boy who slips me
    crumbs of sweet bread
    through a crack in the wall,
    and precious sips of water
    even though I am too weak and too stunned
    to thank him

What a strange
    unexpected answer
    to all my horrified curses
    and prayers

María del Pilar

We rarely see him anymore
    but we hear that she punishes him
    two or three times each week
There are rumors of insanity
    hers or his.

Always hungry, the whisperers say
    a child forced to hide under the table
    to find a few scraps, just like a stray dog.

If only he were a stray,
    then I could find him and feed him,
    my son.

A broken nose from the beatings.
No more golden beak.
A silenced voice.
Or so they imagine.

I know it's not true.
I can hear him singing.
That music of words.
The fluttering wings
Trapped.

TORIBIO

Some things can barely
    be imagined.

At least he has the trade I taught him.
They say his job,
    when he's not being punished,
    is sewing clothes
    of fine linen
    with trimmings.

How is it possible
    that he is no longer a child
    but a man, young and old
    at the same time?

Fifteen or sixteen, more or less
    his verses wasted
    his mind just a feather
    stitched onto someone else's
    fancy hat.

Don Nicolás

~ ~ ~ ~ ~

We let him come to our art lessons.
She lets him watch
   standing
   behind her chair

He never has a chance
   to hold a pencil
   but there is something in his eyes that tells me
   he already knows how to draw
   what he sees
   enormous murals
   filled with stories
   sketched
      in the hot, sunny
      blue air

JUAN

~ ~ ~ ~ ~

The young master Don Nicolás has given me
   a bronze pencil case
   and a stub of crayon

I listen
I watch
I learn how to draw
   eyes and ears
   eyebrows
   lips
   teeth
   a woman running
      with loose, flowing hair, weeping and running
      in a world
      made of wind

JUAN

Again I draw with my stub of crayon
   hiding the act of sketching
   my secret
   even Don Nicolás doesn't know
   what it's like for me
   to live in this house decorated with pictures
   on walls and doors
   ceilings and furniture
      there are paintings everywhere,
      portraits
      landscapes
      murals

Flowers
the fronds of ferns and palm trees
harps, ribbons
   birds in flight
   pleasure gardens where ladies with parasols stroll
   beside peaceful lakes

Those are the things I see
   on the walls
These are the things I draw
   for myself:

bones
the skeletons of infants
men buried with rooster feathers
and weapons
plates filled with food.

The old Africans say those are the things
buried inside these walls
under the murals of pleasure gardens
and parasols.

I am new, not old
I am Cuban, not African
I will not measure my years
by the passing of hurricanes
I do not measure the distance I travel
by counting the number of rooster songs I hear
as I pass
from one farm
to the next.

Instead of the raging, terrifying storm
I will choose to measure its silent, peaceful eye.

Instead of the crowing of roosters
I will make up my mind to count
the songs growing
inside my head.

I am new
    not old.
I am almost tired of drawing
    so many
        hidden
        bones.

LA MARQUESA DE PRADO AMENO

When we are at the country house, I take him fishing
    in the afternoons and cool mornings.

He baits my hook,
    sits on the roots of a wild *guásima* tree
    composing his secret verses
    imagining
    that I do not know.

Such sad rhymes, I tell him,
    even though he has not dared to recite them
    out loud.

They flicker all around him, like fireflies in the night
    stray words arranging their blinking lights
    into some sort of orderly
    rhythm.

The sight of so much invisible music
    makes me sigh.

I warn him again and again: don't make me sad
    with those flickering fireflies
    of rhyme.

Don Nicolás

~ ~ ~ ~ ~

She has him thrashed.
We have to shun him, pretending he does not exist.
She sits him in a chair in the parlor
    with signs posted all around him, warning us
    that we must never speak to him.
She hides behind the curtain
    and listens to make sure
    he doesn't cry.

He knows it will be worse if she sees him weep
    and accuses him of making her sad.
I hope he knows that when this is over
    he will fish with me again,
    and swim with me, and ride horses.
We will pretend we are brothers.

Does he ever dream of galloping away?
Once I asked.
I waited.
He did not answer.
Then I remembered: the bounty hunters.
Wanted posters for runaway slaves
    offering generous rewards.
Guns and dogs tracking men into the wilderness

into the mountains
where there are said to be
whole villages of runaways
living in caves.
Hiding.

JUAN

~ ~ ~ ~ ~

I sit tied and gagged.
She is there, behind the curtain.
The tight cloth choking my mouth keeps me safe.
She can't hear the stories I tell myself in secret.
In silence.
Hidden.

I talk to the tables and walls.
I talk to the people and fruit trees
and horses and fish
in the paintings.

These are the stories I tell in my mind:
Fevers. Scars. Wilderness.

Once, on a day when I was not tied up and gagged,
I took some brushes that Don Nicolás had given me.
I was angry. I painted a witch.
The witch was doctoring a demon,
    healing the demon
    taking care of the demon.
    The witch was happy.
The demon was sorrowful.
Everyone who saw my painting laughed

except Toribio,
my father,
honorable tailor
a good man who wants nothing to do with magic
of the evil sort.

He took my paint brushes away.
Now I have nothing left
    only verses
    and secrets.

LA MARQUESA DE PRADO AMENO

Some people can never be satisfied.
The poet-boy, for instance.
Nothing is ever enough for him.
I have to tell the overseers to teach
   the same lessons
   over and over
   locking his ankles in the stocks
   tying him to a cross like Jesus.
Or tying him to a ladder laid out on the ground
   face down, mouth down
   so he cannot speak
   except to count his own lashes out loud.
And even then, when he loses count
   as they always do when they pass out
   from shameful weakness
Even then, when the overseer makes him start over
   counting again from number one
   until he finally reaches number nine
And even when this is done nine days in a row
   still he bleeds and weeps,
   trying to show me
   that he has won

he has triumphed once again
he has proven that he can still
make me sad.
Evil child.

María del Pilar

Sometimes he runs to us at night
    we hold him while he weeps
    ashamed to cry at his age
    a young man, not a child
    and yet, how could it be any other way
    when he is the only one in our family
    who is not free?

He is still the page at her parties
    he stands behind her chair when she plays cards
    he rides on the back of her carriage
    on the way to the country house
    or the palace of some other noblewoman
    or the theater in Havana
    where she tosses gold and jewels to the actors
    as if they were flowers, not gemstones and pearls.

He clings to the carriage
    holding a lantern all night
    many nights in a row
    until finally it happens
    he falls asleep
    the lantern drops
    he falls.

JUAN

~ ~ ~ ~ ~

Sleep enchants the human spirit.
Each time I fall into dreams
    while holding the lantern
    she sends me once again
    to the stocks
    that trap of splintered, bloodstained wood
    where ankles, neck, and wrists
    are locked in place.

I feel like an ox in its yoke
    except that pairs of oxen are free to move
    pulling the plow
    tearing down trees
    making way for more sugarcane fields
    on this island
    where once
    there were forests of cool, soothing shade
    and clearings of warm
    clear light
    and narrow pathways leading
    away.

Juan

~ ~ ~ ~ ~

My mother comes from her shack
    walking on tiptoes
    until she reaches me
    hand over mouth
    to hide her shock.

Seeing me locked in the stocks
    she whispers son, *ay, mi hijo*, my son
    and it sounds like something mothers
    in many places
    far away
    must have murmured
    many times
    long ago.

Then she tells me
    Toribio is gone
    my father
    is dead.

Together we call to him
    speaking to the air
    not the ground
    not a grave.

DON NICOLÁS

I used to imagine
    that tasting dark foods
    would make me dark like him
    chocolate, molasses, or dark wild honey
    would make my mother
    whip me and lock me in the cellar.

Now I know
    that when she tells him to stand behind her chair
    while she eats or plays cards
    when she tells him to spread his elbows
    to shelter her ears
    from being bumped by clumsy serving girls
    somehow she imagines
    that his dark thoughts
    have seeped into her thoughts
    when really
    it is exactly
    the opposite.

She is the one
    with a mind
    that needs light.

La Marquesa de Prado Ameno

~ ~ ~ ~ ~

I let the sad poet-boy imagine
    that soon he will be free.

That way he learns
    many crafts
    preparing himself
    for the future
    as a tailor
    like his father
    or a pastry chef
    working with sugar and chocolate
    instead of ink.

Juan

I let her imagine
    that I do not have
    an inkwell
    made of eggshell
    given to me
    by her own son
    along with a quill
    for writing secrets
    so that when we've heard the verses
    of some improvisational poet
    at an elegant party
    in the house of a nobleman
    I can take home the rhymes
    I remember
    and change the words to new ones
    making all words
    my own

JUAN

~~ ~~ ~~ ~~ ~~

These rhymes are mine
    mine alone
    never memorized
    or copied
    in any way

Rhymes about
    soaring in spirit
    a spark imprisoned
    bursting its bonds
    of clay

Rhymes about feeling delight
    wrapped in love
    alive
    and able
    to pray

JUAN

Life has its moments of wonder
    and wondering.
These are the pastries
I'm learning to cook in the kitchen,
a kingdom of whispering girls:
    little spiders of ripe fried banana
    round sunsets of sliced oranges and sweet potato
    sticky mountains of coconut and caramel
    and best of all, strange creamy desserts
    from distant lands
    foreign foods with strange names like "Napoleon"
    names that make me want to read or travel
    words that make me long for a chance
    to learn

The kitchen girls whisper about crocodiles
    and water trolls
    sharks, mermaids
    caves
    forests with paths that glow
    paths of moonlight
    showing runaway slaves
    where to run

Later, when part of the sky is rainy
    and part is sunny
    the kitchen girls say that the devil
    is beating his wife
    but who would marry the devil anyway?
    No, that one must not be true.
    You have to watch out
    for other people's whisperings
    so many of them turn out to be
    tall tales
    in other words
    lies.

JUAN

~~ ~~ ~~ ~~ ~~

Sometimes when I am not sewing like my father
   or cooking sweets
   and listening
   to the whispered daydreams
   of kitchen girls
   I have to ride
   on the back of my owner's carriage
   all night
   many nights
   in a row
   until
   I get dizzy
   and fall
   asleep
   and fall
   with the lantern
   and fall
   landing in dreams
   landing in mud

La Marquesa de Prado Ameno

He landed in the road
    the light of the lantern, my lantern
    lost
    even though the lantern itself
    somehow landed upright
    a small miracle of sorts
    pure glass, but not broken
    only one small flame
    extinguished!

He must have known what would happen
    certainly he should know how to prevent falling
    and dropping
    such a fragile glass lantern
    onto the road
    without breaking the glass
    who is he to receive such a gift
    the miracle of only one small flame
    extinguished?

Faster and faster the horses galloped
    as I shouted to the driver, run, run, run
    leave him behind
    make him walk

let him see what it feels like
to be left alone
on life's road
without light!

JUAN

Imagine
   how many directions there are
   all alone
   on dark nights!

I could have walked away, to the mountains.
Even though there are bounty hunters
   with hungry dogs and pointing guns
   aren't there also caves
   for hiding?

I could have walked backward along the dark road
   instead of forward
   who says I have to follow a carriage
   when it leaves me behind?

So I stood there, alone in the darkness and silence
   imagining
   waiting to see what would happen.
He came
   the overseer
   with his whips and chains
   moving swiftly
   to catch me

before I could get away
escaping
into the mouths of hidden caves
or hungry dogs.

Maria del Pilar

Imagine
    how I feel
    seeing him here
    locked in this twisted
    position
    ankles and neck
    in the stocks
    my own son.
So I speak.

Silence!
    Again and again the overseer makes noise
    crying out, giving the command
    for silence

but I speak
to my son
    my own son.

The overseer is so young
    surely he will understand
    he must have a mother
    who speaks
    with love.

The first blow
   of the whip
   on the flesh
   of my son
   enters
   my heart.

Teeth and fists
   shrieking and kicking
   I punch, I attack!

Now we are here together
   both twisted
   and locked
   in our dungeon
   of sorrowful
   hopes.

JUAN

Fireflies, music, angels,
   birds, wings,
   God,
   why?
These are just a few
   of the words I find
   for songs to sing
   and rhymes to rhyme
   while my mother and I
   try to stay alive
   waiting for mercy
   or death
   whichever comes first—
   or are they
   the same?

MARÍA DEL PILAR

~ ~ ~ ~ ~

Soon your movements will be flight, he says
    the air your highway
    this is the promise he quotes for me
    borrowing hope from a verse by Arriaza
    one of his favorite Spanish poets
    pronto tus movimientos vuelo serán
    los aires tu camino . . .
    soon your movements will be flight
    the air your highway . . .

I hold this promise in my secret place
    my place for wishing and listening
    wherever that place
    may be

Soon my movements
    will be flight
    the air my highway . . .

I wait and wait
    for the movement
    of wings
    to begin!

Juan

In the darkness my mother answers my songs
  with her songs
  while we are both tied to a ladder and punished
  nine lashes of the whip
  counting out loud
  nine nights in a row
  strange novena of pain
  instead of the usual novena
  of prayers
  instead of nine rosaries prayed
  for nine nights in a row
  as if someone on earth had
  so arrogantly decided
  that God would not listen
  the first one, two, three, four, five, six, seven,
  eight times!

He listens
  I hear Him
He answers with Psalms whispered
  through the mouth of my mother
  a Psalm about the music of life
  and one about escaping like a bird
  from a hunter's trap . . .

Is it true that King David in ancient Israel
    really wrote such sad-happy doubtful-hopeful
    back-and-forth maybe-someday
    no-not-maybe
    these-are-promises absolutely-definitely
    but-we-have-to-wait
    songs?

MARÍA DEL PILAR

He keeps me alive with his whisperings
   about poets born long ago
   and poets forced to flee for their lives
   and poets catching words in flight
   like wild birds!

How can it be, this survival in chains?
How can it be, this strange vision of truth?
Just look at the overseer, look, it is true
   how can it be that I never really noticed before?
The one with the whip, he is dark
   just like us
   dark and frowning, ashamed,
   that is why he lets Juan
   give me gifts of syllables, words, songs
   old ballads about chivalry and love, my favorites
   also the one about the sailor who sings
   to calm the sea
   when the wind grows still
   fish rise to the surface
   and birds in flight pause
   to listen
   listen
   listen . . .

THE OVERSEER

Strange songs, so strange they almost make me weep
    but of course I can't, I won't.
    I'm not doing anything sad.

This is life, there are people with whips
    and people with scars
    from the lashes.
    Which would you choose?
    Tell me,
    which?

Silence! I shout,
    but the noise goes on and on.
    The boy keeps whispering rhymes
    to comfort his weeping mother.
Lope de Vega, he says, naming a poet
    then whispering the verse,
    something about an angel
    telling a soul
    to come to the window
    and look out . . .

La Marquesa de Prado Ameno

I'm not a fool, I can tell when a rhyme is meant
   to mock me.
So when I learned that the boy
   was comforting his mother
   with lines from verses
   like the one by Garcilaso de la Vega
   about trees bending down
   so the birds
   can listen . . .

Well, just imagine
   how I felt . . .
And then there was the one by Fray Luis de León
   about the heavy cares
   of a man enslaved
   to another man's will . . .

And worst of all
   that dreadful poem
   by Andrés Fernández de Andrade
   about a nightingale
   who prefers its poor nest of feathers
   and straw
   to pleasing the ears

of some famous prince
while held prisoner
in a golden cage . . .

Well, just imagine
the boy even dares to recite the verse
by Pedro Soto de Rojas
a poem I once loved
when I was young and had dreams of my own . . .
but now . . . well . . . now . . .
it's that one, the song to a goldfinch:
You are caged
and I am caged
You sing
and I sing . . .

Hateful boy, hateful verse
how dare he make me remember
what it feels like
to want words
musical words
to yearn and sigh and wish and pray
for a song
of my own!

DON NICOLÁS

~ ~ ~ ~ ~

Someday
    when she's not paying attention
    I'll sneak him away to the city
    where he'll be
    almost free
    and we'll study
    side by side.
Someday . . .

JUAN

~~~ ~~~ ~~~ ~~~ ~~~

I almost feel free
   here in the kitchen
   released from the stocks
   and the whip
   and the eyes
   of the overseer
   as he stands over me,
   seeing
   my suffering

Here in the kitchen, the girls laugh and tease
   they call me silly, and giggle, and say, please
   sing to us, Golden Beak, just one more verse
   to help us dream sweet daydreams
   of peace!

So while they slice and spice and sweeten and ice
   golden pineapples made cold
   by blocks of frozen water
   brought all the way from some distant
   north
   in the hold
   of a ship
   floating,

while they do these amazing, impossible things
    I sing my rhymed daydreams
    of Kings' Day and carnivals

Just imagine, they sigh when I'm finished
how sweet to know that time passes
    the calendar moves
    like a horse
    galloping

Soon it will be Kings' Day!
We would hide piles of straw under our beds
    if we had beds like Don Nicolás and the other
    free children

Just imagine, on the morning of Kings' Day
we would find gifts
    just like the ones the Three Wise Kings
    brought to the baby Jesucristo
    in his straw-softened manger

JUAN

Kings' Day doesn't exist for us
  in the way it exists for them
We have to dance
  at the carnival
We're free to dance
  at the carnival!
We dance in honor
  of the Wise King, the one with dark skin
  does anyone remember his name?

We dance in the streets
  and on the plantations
  the drums are allowed on that day
  the same drums that are hidden
  all year

They let us make costumes
  that mock them
  believe it or not
  costumes so we can make fun of the
  countesses,
  dukes,
  marchionesses

Imagine!
We're even allowed to make fun of
    priests,
    nuns,
    judges,
    and armored conquistadores with uplifted
    ominous swords
We make fun of everyone, light skin or dark
    light heart or heavy
    light sky or cloudy

We make fun of ourselves
We make pain
    feel like fun

Aren't we clever?

JUAN

~ ~ ~ ~

Time passes.
The rest of the calendar
 is just as strange
 as Kings' Day
 our one day of freedom
 to dance.

Holy Week begins on Palm Sunday
 seven days before Easter
Holy Week is the only week
 when women of noble blood
 cannot wear their ghostly mask,
 their pale powder of eggshells and rice
It's the week
 when they have to be humble
 so that even the dark ones
 aren't allowed
 to look light
It's the week when everyone guesses
 whose darkness came
 from the south of Spain
 from Moors as dark
 as Cuban slaves
 and which are dark because

they are
our secret
half sisters, half-slave.

Of all the strange pages
        on this island's unusual calendar
        the one that bothers me most
        comes during the bitter harvest
        of towering, sweet-flavored sugarcane
        delicious syrup encased inside stems
        as tall as a giant
        as thick as an arm
It's the season when canecutters never sleep
        when some of the priests turn their backs and
            allow
        overseers to pretend that Sunday comes
        every ten days
        instead of every seven
It's the season when weary canecutters
        with their blurred vision
        chop off their own limbs
        or drop under the wheels
        of the oxcarts
        or fall into the vats
        of boiling syrup
        or are crushed
        between the stones
        that grind the cane

and separate it from the bagasse
a fancy word
that means dry, fibrous trash
like my heart.

After the harvest, one more carnival, one more dance
one more day
of freedom to pretend
that we are free

and then the Dead Season
the time when there is no cane
to cut
and the field hands are finally
permitted
to sleep.

DON NICOLÁS

I would like to give mournful Juan
　　a reason
　　for smiling
　　here it is, Juanito, my brother
　　(almost)

Yes, of course I mean it, take it, this is yours
　　a coin to spend as you wish
　　one peseta, look, an old coin,
　　no one will mind
　　it's not one of those shiny new coins
　　with the picture of the King of Spain
　　engraved on the silver
　　so you don't have to fret
　　no one will think you are being disrespectful
　　like the slaves who've been whipped
　　or even killed
　　for daring to look directly at
　　colorful wild birds in the forest
　　tocororo birds that wear the same stripes
　　as the uniform
　　of King Fernando
　　don't worry, this is just a coin, not a feather,
　　not a bird.

Take it, Juan, it's just a token
   a gift, let's pretend
   it's Three Kings' Day
   and you are the dark one of those
   Three Wise Kings
   what was his name?

Juan

Last night the young master gave me a coin,
    one peseta
    an old coin
    not a new one bearing the likeness
    of King Fernando
    ruler and monarch of all the provinces
    and colonies of Spain
    including Cuba
    especially Cuba.

Now La Marquesa gives me one of the new coins,
    a pretty one, bright and shiny,
    with the picture of the King.
Give it to that beggar who keeps
    knocking at my door, she commands
    and almost without thinking, I switch the coins
    tossing them lightly from hand to hand
    as I walk toward the door
    open it
    place a coin
    in the palm
    of the beggar.

I do it almost without thinking,

but not completely
because really, isn't it true
that everyone is always thinking,
at least a little bit?

The shiny new coin has inscriptions
so even though its value
as money is the same as the old coin
I see a chance to read
and I take it
a chance to understand
the curls and angles
of mysterious letters,
delightful, adventurous
words.

The coin falls
the new one
intended for the beggar
who has already scurried away
thrilled to be holding my old coin.

Shameless!
La Marquesa cries out
when she sees me grabbing
the bright coin
the one that I've dropped
so now I try to hide it

but the shiny surface
and beautiful picture
and mysterious writing
make me look like I'm trying to lift a golden star
or the silver moon.

Shame!
Shouting and pulling me by the ear,
    she accuses me
    of stealing
    from beggars.

She's right,
    I've stolen,
    I've cheated
    in order to possess strange letters and words,
    letters that don't even make sense,
    so in an odd way she's right:
    I am shameless,
    shameful.
    She's always right.
    Isn't she?
    Or is she?
    Maybe we're both right.
    Is such a thing possible?

La Marquesa de Prado Ameno

How dare he steal my coin,
    leaving me no choice!
    He must be punished at the sugar mill
    that's it,
    I'll send him away for a few days
    or weeks
    or maybe even a few months
    what choice do I have?
    Who wouldn't do the same?

I'll have him dressed in burlap clothes
    they'll tie him to a mule
    and if,
    no, not if, but when—
    when he tries to escape:
    Hah! Just watch
    how easily they'll catch him
    and tie him again.

Just watch,
    not even my pitifully merciful,
    foolishly helpful son Nicolás
    will be able to help him this time!

Just watch,
    even my sickly husband, the Marquis,
    who rarely speaks to anyone
    and is practically invisible in this house,
    even he will try to help that boy,
    claiming Juanito the slave
    is the only one who treats him kindly
    giving him more attention
    than the Marquis gives me
    running all those errands to help the Marquis
    bringing him medicines
    trying to help,
    everyone always trying to help
    except when they should
    be helping me!

JUAN

Nothing to pack before leaving
    nothing to say
    nothing to watch
I close my eyes and feel the things they do to me
    instead of looking
    at the blood
    the bruises
    the pain

First there's the mule, then the boat, now the fields
    and more fields
    endless fields
    of pretty, delicious, sweet, green
    towering sugarcane
    a world of sugar
    waiting
    for the harvest

Out in the fields there are faces
    the faces of slaves
    chopping cane
    faces scratched
    by the razor-sharp leaves
faces trapped

so I keep my eyes closed
it's enough just feeling
their pain

Now I'm shackled, chained, trapped
twenty-five lashes of the whip
in the morning
my breakfast of screams
twenty-five more lashes at noon
instead of lunch
I taste my tears
I eat shame

Nine days in a row
the overseer almost apologizes
her instructions, he says, I have no choice
and anyway, nine is a good number
women who pray *la novena*
pray for nine days in a row
just like this
only your prayers aren't words
just those moans

He sighs with compassion, the overseer
saying there's no choice, he works hard
he has to please La Marquesa
even though nine days of whipping and moaning
it's too much

too much for both of us
my pain, my fears
and his guilt, the screams and moans reaching
his ears

Merciful.
It's a word
I truly understand now
compassion
kindness

Secretly, the overseer stops whipping
and listening to my moans
long before number nine
is it possible that he can't count?

At the moment it doesn't really matter to me
whether the mercy,
compassion,
and kindness of the overseer
are his own idea
or something that came from an angel of God
maybe the angel
placed a vision in the overseer's mind
a winged picture
of what it would feel like
if his eyes were closed

nine days in a row
and I was the one with the whip,
watching and listening
while he moaned . . .

JUAN

When it's over I struggle to work hard
    trying to please
    the angel of God who sends visions of mercy,
    and trying to please this strange man too
    this watching, listening overseer
    who chose or was chosen
    to leave me
    alive

Nine days, it would have been too much
    I would have shriveled down to nothing
    just a dry wisp
    of my living self
    smaller than those tiny letters engraved
    on a coin
    above the crown
    of the King
    of Spain
    and all her colonies
    especially this island, bittersweet island
    of sugar
    and dreams

María del Pilar

Every time I manage to find poor Juan
   working and working
   out in the fields
   he tells me
   how La Marquesa always promises
   to kill him

So I answer
   with one small truth
   and while I'm speaking
   I can feel the small truth growing
   bigger and bigger
   inside my mouth
   God is good
   and good is always more powerful
   than evil
   I don't know why the devil
   even bothers
   to fight

JUAN

~~ ~~ ~~ ~~

When I'm not in the fields
   and I need to forget
   I can fold shapes of paper
   and paint them
   I can make frames of wild cane
   I can cut out the pictures of people
   from playing cards
   paper dolls
   I give them to children

I figure out how to make shadow puppets
   for slave children
   who love to see how
   lifeless puppets of wood
   learn to dance

Then I'm back indoors again,
   trapped in the fearfully lifeless house
   that will never learn how
   to dance like a home

I fight duels with poets, famous ones who visit
   there's a poet who can wiggle his ears

and one who challenges me to finish his verses
after he leaves the words soaring
like birds in midair

You've won, they tell me,
    Poeta-Esclavo, you've won
    and it feels good,
    how they've turned the words *poet* and *slave*
    into a name, first name and last name so that
    when a man is my friend
    he only uses the first part
    calling me Poet
    not Slave

Don Nicolás

Ay, *no*, not again, *ay no*,
   look, *mira*, he's done it again
   Poet, how could you?
   look what you've done
just imagine
   the risk
just imagine
   what she is capable of doing to your body
   your mind and your soul
just imagine the heart or the non-heart
   of my own mother
   a sad, dancing puppet-woman
think what she will do
   when she sees how your thumbnail
   has carved shapes that look
   like whole letters, whole words
   into the succulent skin
   of this geranium leaf
   releasing
   the fragrance
   of verse

JUAN

This time it's worse than before
    even though I never imagined such a thing
    could be possible
    pain worse than death
    here I am,
    still alive
    but sharing this locked room
    with the dead

She made them lock me inside this dark place
    all alone
    with no one but these cadavers
    for company
    dead bodies everywhere
    cold and naked, all of us,
    in a land of heat
    where we should be outdoors
    covered with green growing blankets of leaves
    in this land of flowers and birds
    paradise
    except for the shackles
    and eyes

so many eyes
eyes of the dead
staring
   staring
      staring

Do they know?
   Do they hate me?
   Can they see
   that I am
   still alive
   just barely?

Bodies seem to rise all around me
   roaming the room
   back and forth

So I stand
   afraid to lie down
   close my eyes
   rest

A broken shutter bangs
   I hear water
   a river
   a ditch
   a torrent falling over a cliff

Each time the shutter opens
    I imagine that one more spirit
    has entered
    this room
Each time it slams shut I know that I am trapped
    just one more visible example
    of death

THE OVERSEER

I turn the key in the lock.
I enter the room in this abandoned infirmary,
   hideous hospital where fifty beds
   meant for the living
   are used by the dead.

Who killed them? Why so many?
   Is it the whippings I give them?
   No, please, God, no, anything but that!

I have a timid assistant who follows me in,
   and an administrator too.
   Look at us: we are officials, we are safe,
   and yet
   there's this smell, and the silence,
   the absence of breath.
We cover our mouths with clean linen handkerchiefs,
   our initials embroidered in the corners, so elegant.
We speak through the cloth, we tie his hands,
   just like the hands
   of our Lord Jesucristo on
   the cross.

Suddenly I wonder,
    what does it mean
    to be saved
    from someone
    like me?

Then we lift him.
    We place his feet in two holes in a board;
    we tie them together, now he's even
    more trapped than before.

Before we leave him, I see blood and the mercy
    of unconsciousness.
    He seems to sleep;
    the sight of his peacefulness
    makes me pray
    that he will not enter
    my dreams
    tonight
    along with all these others,
    the dead,
    his companions.

María del Pilar

My wounded son is in my arms,
   in the chapel,
   weeping

I weep too
Who would not?

Even the overseer weeps
   but only for
   his own soul

And the priest
   has also shed a few tears
   of confusion
   now he tells me to leave

What choice do I have?
   I obey

La Marquesa de Prado Ameno

~~~ ~~~ ~~~ ~~~ ~~~

In the morning I ask if he has been treated well
    and the administrator takes me to see him
    in the chapel.

What a sight!
    I smile and ask him,
    do you want to take
    one more leaf
    of my scented geranium
    and see what will happen
    if you keep trying to scribble
    those meaningless
    words
    with the tip
    of your filthy, soil-stained
    fingernail?

The poet-boy, poet-man,
    almost grown and still composing sad verses
    he says nothing at first,
    then finally,
    with a sigh,
    the proper answer:
    No.

Already he begins to swell like a corpse,
   disgusting,
   a horror
So I command the priest
Bathe him, I say
Apply ointments,
   take care of this poor child
Don't you know how to be merciful
and kind?

JUAN

For three days I am nowhere
    I do not exist
For three more days I am somewhere
    in pain

At night my mother sneaks in and helps me learn
    how to walk on wounded legs
She tells me she has enough money
    to purchase my freedom

I remind her that our first owner already set me free

She cannot think of an answer,
    we both know it's true
    I'm already free
    in this land of dreams and legends
    island
    of fantasies
    where I almost
    exist

JUAN

~ ~ ~ ~ ~

I weep, I work, I wait,
   and then once again
   I'm accused

This time it's one tiny game hen
   that's missing
I am innocent
   but who will believe me?
So I tell the same truth
   over and over
   If I were brave enough to steal
   I would take myself
   and some books,
   not a bird!

THE OVERSEER

This time I tie him with rope and make him run
    in front of my horse,
    in front of two hungry, obedient dogs,
    in front of the hooves
    and the claws
    and the fangs
    and my whip.

Watch him fall!
    Now I speak to the dogs;
    watch them turn
    into wolves.

See how the teeth
    enter his cheek
    sinking in
    all the way
    to his molars.
    There are fangs in his legs too,
    look at the left one.
    What a shame
    if he is hurt so badly
    that he will never
    be able to walk.

I grab the rope,
I yank it to save him
    proud of my compassion
    and at the same time furious with him
    for dislocating his arm
    at the end of my rope.

Why does everything with him
    always have to be
    so complicated?

JUAN

The worst is over, I imagine,
    I hope
    now I'm walking again,
    on these bleeding legs
    walking and walking
    until we finally reach the sugar mill
    where I will rest
    in the stocks
    while receiving my twenty-five
    lashes

Seven officials gather around me,
    demanding answers
    do they imagine that the overseer
    will dare to let me go
    if I tell the truth again and again?
    or do they imagine that I will be released
    if I try a few lies
    and claim that I took the missing game hen:
    I ate it
    the meat was tender
    my belly is full?
    or what about this one:
    I took it to sell

so that I could buy a fancy hat
for courting the sweet, pretty girls?

I choose the hat,
and seven officials now want to see it
but there is no hat
only the one
I imagined
so I say I bought shoes,
but I have no shoes
the questions and answers go on and on
I tell a thousand and one lies
trying to save myself
from the torment

JUAN

Seven thousand stories for the seven officials,
    then eight thousand,
    nine thousand,
    ten
    but none of my fantasies are false enough
    to rescue me
    from these people who keep shouting:

TELL THE TRUTH!

So instead of speaking I begin to dream
    of the various saints' opinions
    on the location of paradise
    east, west, north, south,
    up, always up,
    never down

I dream of my mother and brothers
    free in their small bell-shaped hut
    thatched with singing, wind-rustled,
    dry leaves of palm
    they are free
    so am I
    more or less

I dream of streets, narrow and shady
    to protect the people walking on them
    from sun
    cobblestone streets that follow the directions
    of the four invisible winds
    I see the winds flying
    escaping from
    town

JUAN

~~ ~~ ~~ ~~ ~~

The nine nights of terror and dreaming are over
    because finally a brave muleteer has admitted
    that he saw the steward eating a game hen

So now I am free, in a sense
    free to work, and my jobs are these:
    forgetting to dream while I drive the oxen,
    burn the cane,
    press the juice of sweet sugar
    into a syrup
    of courage

Forgetting the truth while I carry the sugar
    walking even though my leg is damaged
    and I cannot
    walk

Forgetting anger while I place cones of sugarloaf
    in a shed

Forgetting,
    the hardest form of work
    and then suddenly, as swift as lightning
    disaster again

here it comes
a piece of the roof of the shed
as it falls,
I leap to escape death
even though I can't forget that death
was the thing I wished for every second
of those long, strange nine days

The slave standing beside me
stacking cones of sugarloaf in the shed by my side
has been crushed.

His name is Andrés.
He was born on this island,
a native
like me.
His name was Andrés.

María del Pilar

Twice his freedom has been promised
   this time I paid,
   yet the act is denied
   I've been tricked,
   I'm a fool
   but after seeing
   the crushed skull
   and scraped skin
   and broken eyes
   of Andrés
   I knew I was right
   to try

Don Nicolás

My friend is sick in his spirit,
  his wounded soul
  his sorrowful heart
His brothers have spoken to me
  they beg me each day,
  please seek mercy
Don't be like your mother

So I take him back into the house
  where his only job is forgetting
  still, he will not eat
  or play with the children who call to him,
  begging for silly verses and fables
  and tales of imaginary
  heroes

All he does is weep while he works
  polishing his mind to clean it,
  trying to forget
  while he polishes the smooth wood
  of my mother's carved mahogany furniture

Now he has a hat and shoes,
  the ones I've given him

a hat and shoes just like
the ones he invented

I must have dreamed them out loud, he says
my voice
made them real

JUAN

Can it be, is this true, O merciful Lord,
   did you actually hear my prayers and the begging
   of my brothers?

Suddenly I belong
   to Don Nicolás
   instead of his mother
   and he says I am his son
   not his slave
   even though
   we are the same age
   more or less

Miracles amaze me
watch how he pays me
   with coins
watch how he lets me buy cures
   for my fever, my cough
   a brew of cactus fruit and poppies
   orange blossoms, poplar leaves, milk and honey
   then dried beef mixed
   with chocolate
   for strengthening
   the lungs

DON NICOLÁS

He mends my clothes
    cleans my shoes
    tidies my room
    arranges my day
    my surroundings
    my desk

His affection for me
    knows no bounds
    and I know
    that it's only because
    he peeks
    at my books

JUAN

Almost free
   more or less
   just imagine:
   I am not allowed
   to go out alone
   or step into the kitchen
   where maids and cooks
   speak of indecent things
   but in all other ways I am free
   more or less

I tidy his chair, his desk, his books
   I give him a haven
   where he can study

I long to write
   so I use my new coins
   to buy quills and fine paper
   for tracing his words

Secretly I practice
   penmanship
   syllables
   symbols

letters that scatter
strange, wondrous meanings
across the wide world

I even copy the titles of paintings
until I am caught
then I pull out some sewing
and begin
to mend

At night when everyone else is asleep
I take a stub of candle
and copy the intricate verses of poets
whose long noble names are enclosed
in thick books

I write and rewrite and recite
every dream
along with a few
simple rhymes
of my own

Don Nicolás

I am ready
   to be married
   to Doña Teresa de Herrera

So I give Juan the tailor
   doubloons of gold
   each time he carries
   one of my secretive messages
   of love

María del Pilar

Suddenly my dear son is able to send
   so much money
   but is he free?
They've moved him to Guanajay where he sews
   for the bride of his master
They say God has given my son a strange gift
   not of verse but of hands
   the ability to stitch silken cloth
   and to heal
   wounded flesh

Suddenly he is famous
   for curing
   the ill

Counts and Countesses
   Dukes and Duchesses
   everyone sends for him
   whenever pain and fear
   are suffered

Juan

Agony either makes a person want more pain
   for others
   or none at all
   for anyone
   anywhere
   any time

So I've learned to give baths
   of warm herbs and roots
   my vigils at bedsides
   are faithful
   I pray

And even though no one knows that I've learned
   how to write
   I do it
   I write
   every word
   that is moaned
   by my impatient
   patients
   as they wait
   to be healed

I keep a written record of the spitting and snoring
    the soundness of sleep
    and all the other things
    that should not be mentioned
    except in the presence
    of doctors
    and God

They come in the morning
    the doctors who praise my attention to details
    no matter how foul-scented, tragic, or hideous

I am famous
    but is fame
    a blessing
    or curse?

La Marquesa de Prado Ameno

He is famous
 and best of all
 he is mine.

I don't care how absurdly
 my son and his bride
 try to argue.

I have sent
 for the boy wizard
 the healer
 the mysterious wordsmith
 the slave
 he is mine.

Juan

~ ~ ~ ~ ~

I try everything I can think of
    begging
    pleading
    even a formal request to the magistrate
    written documents
    petitioning my transfer
    to a new master

She warns me to stop trying to talk
    to the priest and the courts

Have I ever harmed you? she asks
    in front of witnesses,
    so I'll know
    what I'm expected to say
    and to do

How dare you remember your mother, she says
    I am your mother
    this is your home

So once again I pretend
    that love and nature
    and logic

have all been replaced
by this nightmare
a vision
strange life
lost in dreams

JUAN

One morning a rooster comes into the house
    and sings in my ear
    strange life

One day a free man insults my mother
    I fight
    unafraid of the lashes
    the pain

Day after day I hear conch shells blown
    as trumpets
    calling the field slaves to work before dawn
    grabbing their machetes for chopping the cane
    long sharp blades, so useless
    against guns

One day I run from the garden
    I hide
    in a swamp
    on the road
    to a castle
    strange feeling
    this courage
    this hope

JUAN

I walk to the castle and tell my story, asking for help
The Count of Jibacoa swears he will protect me
Soon those who know me,
 poets, scholars, doctors, priests
 step forth to defend me
 but a deputy comes

I am tied, draped in burlap
 they take my shoes, shave my head
 drag me back to the fields where I work
 side by side
 with these men who are marked
 by the shapes of their tribes
 carvings of stars, suns, and moons on dark cheeks
 teeth filed to points
 like the fangs of the lions they killed
 when they were warriors
 before the ships came and bought them
 from Arab slave traders who bought them
 from their own kings
 or the enemies
 who'd captured them
 in battle
 strange world

Juan

~ ~ ~ ~ ~

At night there are shooting stars, fireflies,
    wide-awake dreams
    I think of all the stories kitchen girls told me
    when I was little
    about mermaids dancing on waves
    trolls in the rivers
    tiny wishing wells
    GIANT WISHES
and I think of my mother reciting the songs
    of King David
    the one about a heart overflowing
    with a beautiful thought
    the one about a tongue like the pen
    of a skillful poet

I think of daily life
    stories of slaves who somehow ran away
    to secret forests
    hiding
    like pirates
    in villages
    surrounded
    by the magic
    of songs

La Marquesa de Prado Ameno

~ ~ ~ ~ ~

This time his punishment for running away is only
   nine days.

Then I fetch him and give him fine clothing
   again.

Then I take him to town in the coach
   like a prince
   more or less
   sitting beside the coachman
   practically
   a seat of honor.

Now we will see
   if he will be
   at least a little bit grateful
   this time
   at least a tiny bit grateful
   to me!

JUAN

~ ~ ~ ~

Here I am in the house again
  hiding behind doors,
  reading books,
  all the poetry of San Juan de la Cruz
  poet-saint, prisoner, exile
  tortured, tormented, disbelieved, persecuted
  yet somehow the words,
  a strange fountain of hope:
  Apártalos, amado, que voy de vuelo . . .
  Look away, beloved, I'm going to fly . . .

and these words:
  A las aves ligeras,
  leones, ciervos, gamos saltadores,
  montes, valles, riberos,
  aguas, aires, ardores,
  y miedos de las noches veladores . . .
  O birds on easy wings,
  lions, stags, leaping fallow deer,
  mountains, valleys, shores,
  waters, winds, passions,
  and terror in the watchful nights . . .

and these words, strangest of all
   strangely easy to understand:
   Saber no sabiendo . . .
   To know without knowing . . .

To know without knowing
   a life filled with dreams
   heaven unseen
   strange faith, strangely real
   strangely mysterious fountain of words
   source of hope

So I let my mind fly
   free thoughts lifting, unseen
   up, up, up to the inviting
   unknown

JUAN

~~~ ~~~ ~~~ ~~~ ~~~

Out in the night
   slaves are dancing and drumming and singing.
   I smile
   then I cry
   in this house
   always hiding
   like a child
   behind doors
   book in hand.

Juan

One day an artist comes to the house
  to paint flowers
  on an old glass display case
  he asks me to help
  and I do
  with delight
  unafraid to be caught shading roses
  with the magic
  of a brush

When he is finished he gives me a doubloon
  unaware that slaves are gambling out in the sheds
  I accept

Soon she comes, so ferocious, such strange hands,
  a wild search
  soon she finds the doubloon,
  sorrowful payment
  for roses
  fragrant flowers
  stench of doom

LA MARQUESA DE PRADO AMENO

~~~ ~~~ ~~~ ~~~ ~~~

How strangely he seems to have taken
   my sanity
   as if he were the master
   and I the slave
All my thoughts are of punishment
   but after nine days
   or ten
   eleven at most
   he comes back
   because I bring him,
   I fetch him,
   I almost apologize
   more or less
   as if I have allowed him to become
   the only person that matters
   in this, my strange life

He is in the fields
   being punished
   when the news comes
   about his mother
   so unexpected
   such a shock

So I send for him and tell him the sad news
    then I give him three whole coins
    for the priest
    to say a mass
    for her soul

JUAN

How can I believe this?
   No, of course not,
   such a thing is not possible.
My mother gone
   nothing left
   but this old empty box
   in my hands
   the inheritance she left for me
   empty space
   enclosed
   by four small
   wooden walls.

So I find the secret compartment
   and inside I discover three bracelets of gold
   two rosaries, a crucifix
   a few dirty trinkets of coral
   and some paper:
      official documents proving
      that La Marquesa owed her money
      more than enough to purchase
      my freedom
      even though it has already been paid for
      and ignored.

Who could have guessed?
    That my mother owned a horse, then a colt,
    then more
    all of them sold to my owner
    in an effort to save enough wealth
    for me to purchase official documents proving
    that I own
    myself.

LA MARQUESA DE PRADO AMENO

How dare he ask to keep her things
    and collect her debts
    as if a mere slave could expect to receive
    an inheritance!

I tell him I am the heir of my slaves
    I say all you have belongs
    to me!

Then I add:
    If you speak of her money to me again
    you will never see
    moonlight or sunlight or stars!

Now go
    I command you
    this is my house
    see how it is filled with fine
    mahogany furniture
    from the forests
    of this lovely island?

Go, polish the wood,
    enjoy your freedom

to move through this house,
cleaning fine furniture
instead of rotting
in a dark, airless room
with dead bodies!

Juan

I long for wings
   to fly away

The gold is my mother's
   a gift of love

I take her bracelets
   to the church

I sell them
   to buy candles

Airy flames
   a gift of love

For my mother's
   spirit

My prayers
   a fragrance

of words
   flying to God

Don Nicolás

What was he thinking,
   defying my mother?
   what did he expect?
   taking the gold bracelets
   selling them
   burning those candles
   all the gold bracelets vanishing
   strange alchemy
   worked in reverse
   changing jewelry
   to flames
   rising from candles
   flight of air
   life of dreams
   melting wax

JUAN

~ ~ ~ ~ ~

Prison, of course,
   no matter that the bracelets
   should have been
   mine

A kind man comes
   and sets me free
   he shares his food
   and lets me sleep
   in the stable
   with horses,
   dreaming
   of wild manes
   and flying hooves

Soon La Marquesa comes to visit
   and the kind man has to put me
   in chains
Pretend, he whispers,
   pretend you have suffered the whip
   and the work
   and the weeping
   she expects

When nine days have passed
  she brings me a new set of elegant clothes

How weary I am of being rescued
  by my tormentor!

La Marquesa de Prado Ameno

~ ~ ~ ~ ~

I tell him to throw himself at my feet
I command him to beg my forgiveness
I order him to sit at my table and eat

His mouth never opens
   he won't speak, won't swallow

I'll send you fishing, I promise
   we'll go to the circus, together
   we'll see the funny clowns and the flying acrobats!

Still nothing, no verses, no words from the child
   or is he a man now?

Look, I'll let you study,
   you'll ride through the hills with my sons,
   you can gallop,
   how free and how fine
   you will feel!

His silence is torment.
   How dare he refuse
   to meet my eyes, smile, eat my food,
   give me thanks!

Don Nicolás

Ah, Mother, my mother, how oddly she speaks,
   making him stand behind her
   while she plays those wild games
   of cards
   then giving him
   every coin
   she has won
   each and every coin
   without even counting
   her winnings

Can't she see, doesn't she hear
   his silent protests, feel the sharp edges
   of that look
   in his knifelike,
   wounded eyes?

All he wanted was candles
   to burn
   in the church,
   candles for God
   not this pile
   of gold
   won by gambling

JUAN

~ ~ ~ ~

I feel like a homing pigeon
    longing for my dovecote
    Havana is in my heart
    city of poets
    city of freedom
    streets of words
    alleys of wonder
    busy marketplace
    of ideas
    written and spoken
    shared and daydreamed
    embraced or rejected
    replaced or loaded
    onto the wings
    carried home

JUAN

~~~~~~~

La Marquesa seems to be noticing
   for the first time
   that I know how to sew my own clothes
   cook fancy pastries
   teach children their letters
   help them play with scraps of paper
   folding the treasure
   of discarded wrappers and letters to make
   flowers, seashells, pineapples, coins
   each folded papery shape so nearly weightless
   that it can be carried aloft
   by the gentlest suggestion
   of wind

JUAN

~ ~ ~ ~ ~

Poets, painters, doctors, actors,
   singers, sculptors, playwrights,
   lawyers, gentlemen,
   scoundrels, noblemen,
   artisans,
   all are invited; they come, eat, play card games,
   sit at her table, laugh and gossip,
   recite monologues,
   whisper secrets,
   hand me books
   when no one is looking,
   smuggled verses
   for me to read
   like a frightened child
   hidden
   in the silence
   of that dim space
   behind
   every open
   door

Later I copy the smuggled poems
   then set them aside
   and write verses of my own

and whenever La Marquesa is not angry
I try to treat her as kindly
as she imagines her words,
her gifts and actions toward me,
have always deserved

Strange possession
these other secret words, gifts, and actions
the ones I create
in my mind
for myself

JUAN

~ ~ ~ ~ ~

I think of my mother's Psalms of faith
   a single prayer
   and even the excited words of kitchen girls
   believing so many different things
   all at the same time
   saints, mermaids,
   Lord of Lords,
   river trolls,
   one God, many demons,
   one love, many hatreds,
   on and on
   always decided
   and undecided
   at the same time
   always heated
   by fiery new
   possibilities

My verses are icy
   no warmth
   no love

Yet somehow I sell them
   strangers come

from far away
to buy each silly
thing I say
empty rhymes
for troubled times
empty heart
meaningless art

JUAN

~~~~~

Havana is only twelve leagues away
    from this palace of wishes
    where I am the weaver of fairy tales,
    turning straw into gold with my words
    gold for strangers
    straw for myself.

I feel like a carpenter carving puppets
    of rhyme
    wooden words
    not true verses
    not alive
    like true rhymes
    of hope
    and love.

JUAN

There is a girl who lives close by
   angelic Muse
   I give her flowers
   the ones called marvel-of-Peru

She gives me candy, her smile, fresh fruit
   and one kiss
   the kind that sets
   enchanted frog-princes
   free

I tell her the truth
   I tell her I am free

No more stony palace of wishes
   for me

My verses are born now
   alive
   so new

No need to write them on flimsy paper
   how could my heart ever forget
   anything so true?

JUAN

~ ~ ~ ~

Love is not enough
   to end the strange reality
   of a strangely lived
   life

This is how it happens:
   I go to the stream to bathe
   as always
   far from the country house
   far out of view

La Marquesa sends for me and says,
   who gave you permission
   to bathe?

No one, I answer
Then why? she demands
To be clean, I say calmly

The blow is a fierce one, the fist of a beast
   smashing my nose, crushing the bone
   opening two spurting fountains
   of blood

When her noblewoman's delicate fist has completed
　　its secretive labor,
　　destruction,
　　then she calls for men
　　to take my shoes, shave my head,
　　make me carry a barrel of water
　　up a hill
　　over and over; I try but I fall
　　until both the barrel and I end up
　　splashing
　　spilling
　　rolling
　　spitting blood
　　into the stream

Juan

The night is dark
    no moon
    curtains of rain
    heavy gloom

I've never done it before but now
    I lift
    a saddle
    onto
    a horse

On my knees
    in the mud
    I pray
    Lord I trust
    this strange life
    of mine
    to the unknown

I put on a hat
    mount the horse
    ride away

The last thing I hear
    is a voice
    God be with you
    hurry, hurry,
    don't delay!

At first I think I must be imagining
    the voice
Then I realize I'd imagined
    I was hidden by darkness, gloom, and rain

Now I know
    now I see
    through the gloom
    many watch me
    many slaves
    and many free
    dark and light and in-between
    all are praying
    many voices
    many languages
    from Africa
    and all the various
    dialects of Spain
    many voices
    praying for me

So many voices
    wishing me well, crying out
    God be with you
    hurry, hurry
    don't delay!

So many voices, joined as one
    so many eyes in the gloom
    seeing through darkness
    watching me, singing out hopefully
    as I escape!

Acknowledgments

I am deeply grateful to Juan Francisco Manzano for having written poems that haunt me.

I will always be thankful to a generous God, my patient family, and the First Amendment to the U.S. Constitution, for giving me the peace of mind and the physical and intellectual freedom to write about Manzano's life and his poetry.

I wish to express profound respect and warm gratitude to Reka Simonsen for her gentle yet perceptive editorial suggestions, and for believing in this manuscript from the start, and giving it a home.

A hug to Robin Tordini for pulling my manuscript out of the "slush pile" and placing it in Reka's hands.

Admiration and gratitude to Sean Qualls for his artistic genius.

Many thanks to the entire friendly staff at Henry Holt for their treasured support and assistance, especially the copy editor, Deirdre Hare Jacobson, and the designer, Patrick Collins.

I am indebted to the following resources for factual information:

1. *Biblioteca Básica de Autores Cubanos*. "Juan Francisco

Manzano." Obras. Instituto Cubano Del Libro, Clasificación Biblioteca Nacional: 928.60.

2. *Autobiography of a Slave/Autobiografía de un Esclavo, a Bilingual Edition.* By Juan Francisco Manzano. Introduction and modernized Spanish version by Ivan A. Schulman. Translated by Evelyn Picon Garfield. Detroit: Wayne State University Press, 1996.

3. *The Life and Poems of a Cuban Slave: Juan Francisco Manzano.* Edited by Edward J. Mullen. North Haven, Conn.: Archon Books, 1981.

HISTORICAL NOTE

The life of Juan Francisco Manzano haunted me for years before I finally realized that to do justice to the Poet Slave's story, I needed to write it in verse.

Juan often said that he hoped to write a novel about his life. He never had the chance. In fact, strict censorship by the colonial Spanish government prevented all Cuban poets and novelists from writing verses or stories about slavery.

The life story of Juan Francisco Manzano is known only because some of his autobiographical notes were smuggled to England, where they were published by abolitionists who hoped to raise support for their cause.

Unfortunately, the second half of Juan's brief autobiography was lost in transport. As a result, little is known about the years after his courageous escape on horseback. We do know that he lived as a fugitive in Havana for many years, attending poetry readings and publishing books of his own poems while still officially a runaway slave. He married Delia, a mixed-race woman he called his Muse, for her beauty and her ability to play the piano inspired him to write verse. Her parents objected to the marriage because Juan's skin was darker than hers and because he was still technically a slave.

Eventually, Juan used his own income, along with collections taken up by friends and colleagues, to purchase his freedom, even though it had already been granted by his first owner and paid for by his mother.

Admired both as a poet and an honest man, Juan Francisco Manzano also gained fame as a confectioner, using the candymaking skills he'd learned while enslaved. At various times he worked as a tailor, painter, and cook, all trades he'd learned before attaining his freedom.

Then, in 1844, a year that became known as Cuba's Año del Cuero (Year of the Lash), false rumors of a slave rebellion resulted in the arrest of hundreds of people of all races, including many slaves and many poets.

Poetry has always been a powerful force in Latin American history, and poets have been regarded by dozens of governments, including the Spanish colonial one, as dangerous. This perception has arisen because so many poets choose to describe simple truths that affect both the emotions and the social awareness of readers and listeners.

During Juan Francisco Manzano's lifetime, Cubans gathered in homes to hear him read his poems. Those who knew how to read bought his books. People who could not read listened, memorized, and recited his words of hope. Poetry was as much a part of daily life then as television is now.

Because of his ability to influence people, Juan was arrested on charges of trying to stir up a slave rebellion. He had written nothing treasonous, and no actual rebellion had occurred, but Juan and many other Cuban poets were victims of a general atmosphere of fear and suspicion created by the chaos following a series of disastrous hurricanes. With mansions in ruins and crops destroyed, wealthy planters imagined that slaves would take advantage of the confusion to kill them and take over farms. Rumors based on these fears led to the mass execution of innocent poets who had done nothing more than express their feelings in verse.

Juan Francisco Manzano was one of the fortunate few who survived. He was released from prison in 1845. By then, it was clear that there had never been any plans for a rebellion. This tragic period in Cuban history is referred to as the Escalera Conspiracy, named for the ladders where slaves and poets were tied while being whipped.

Even though he survived, Juan was undoubtedly shocked, saddened, and terrified by his year in prison. His brilliant voice was silenced. If he wrote any more verses during the remaining nine years of his life, he must have kept them secret, because none were published. Those years of silence are a powerful testimony to the horror of censorship. Nevertheless, the poetic genius and dramatic life story of Juan Francisco Manzano, the Poet Slave of Cuba, provide us with an even more powerful and inspiring testimony to the ultimate triumph of freedom.

The Poetry of Juan Francisco Manzano

The following are a few examples of Juan Francisco Manzano's capacity for hope. His verses show how he was determined to find beauty and goodness in a world filled with hideous cruelty.

Each excerpt is presented first in the original, rhymed, nineteenth-century Spanish, and then in my own modernized translation. I have attempted to retain the mood and meaning instead of the meter and rhyme.

1. An excerpt from "Dreams" ("Ilusiones"):

*Sí, yo la ví una noche . . . ¡Cuán hermosa
Me pareció esta vez entre otras bellas!
Mas de un afecto tierno que hasta entonces
Ignoraba me fue—sentí en el alma
La dulce agitación del seno
El plácido latir, y el grato anhelo
De vivir para amar y ser dichoso . . .*

Yes, I saw her one night . . . How beautiful
She seemed to me this time, as always!
And from a tender affection up until then
Ignored—I felt in my soul
The sweet agitation of breath

The quiet pulse, and the pleasant desire
To live for love and to be happy . . .

2. An excerpt from "My Thirty Years" ("Mis treinta
   años") shows how even moments of discouragement
   can be a source of awareness of one's own strength:

Cuando miro el espacio que he corrido
desde la cuna hasta el presente día,
tiemblo y saludo a la fortuna mía
más de terror que de atención movido.

Sorpréndeme la lucha que he podido
sostener contra suerte tan impía,
si tal llamarse puede la porfía
de mi infelice ser al mal nacido . . .

—— —— ——

When I look back at the distance I've run
from the cradle to this present day,
I tremble and greet my fortune
more with terror than polite attention.

I marvel at the struggle I've managed
to endure against such drastic luck,
if it can even be called luck, this persistent
unhappiness of one so poorly born . . .

3. An excerpt from "The Firefly Hunter" ("La cocuyera") describes the Cuban tradition of capturing fireflies and wearing them as living hair ornaments, or keeping them in cages used as lanterns. This poem makes us wonder about the true nature of inner freedom, represented by the firefly's flashing light, sometimes visible and sometimes hidden:

Un incauto cocuyo
Revolaba brillando
Ya del prado a la selva.
Ya de la selva al prado.
Libre cual mariposa
Hendiendo el aire vago,
Liba en virgenes flores
Jugos almibarados
Ora esplende, ora oculta
Del fósforo inflamado
La luz a que no cabe
Color acomodado.
¡Cómo vuela invisible!
Lucero es ya bien claro:
Si puesto se oscurece,
Presto ilumina el campo. . . .

～～～

A careless firefly
circled, flickering
from the meadows to the forest.

Then from the forest to the meadow.
As free as a butterfly
wandering through the air,
sipping the juicy nectar
of fresh flowers
sometimes splendid,
sometimes hidden
the glowing flame
of a light that does not end
in a certain color.
Invisible, it flies!
The morning star is bright:
but when it sets
there is darkness,
and when it rises the land
is illuminated. . . .

Further Exploration

Please visit macteenbooks.com for a Teacher's Guide that includes discussion questions, guidelines for creating your own poetry, tips for conducting historical research, and advice for creating your own artistic response to the story.

GO**FISH**

MARGARITA ENGLE

What did you want to be when you grew up?
I wanted to be a wild horse.

When did you realize you wanted to be a writer?
As a child, I wrote poetry. Stories came much later. I always loved to read, and I think that for me, longing to write was just the natural outgrowth of loving to read.

What's your first childhood memory?
When I was two, a monkey pulled my hair at the Havana Zoo. I remember my surprise quite vividly.

What's your most embarrassing childhood memory?
When I was very little, we lived in a forest. I wandered around a hunter's cabin, and found a loaded gun behind a door. I remember feeling so terribly ashamed when people yelled at me for pointing the gun at them. I had no idea I was doing anything wrong.

What's your favorite childhood memory?
Riding horses on my great-uncle's farm in Cuba.

As a young person, who did you look up to most?
Growing up in Los Angeles, I participated in civil rights marches. I admired Martin Luther King Jr. I was also a great fan of Margaret Mead. I wanted to travel all over the world, and understand the differences and similarities between various cultures.

What was your worst subject in school?
Math and PE. I was a klutz in every sport, and I needed a tutor to get through seventh-grade algebra. In high school, my geometry teacher crumpled my homework, threw it on the floor, stepped on it, and said, "This is trash!"

What was your best subject in school?
English. I loved reading, and I loved writing term papers.

What was your first job?
Cleaning houses.

How did you celebrate publishing your first book?
Disbelief, and then scribbling some more.

Where do you write your books?
I do a lot of my writing outdoors, especially in nice weather.

Where do you find inspiration for your writing?
Old, dusty, moldy, tattered, insect-nibbled history books, and the stories my mother and grandmother used to tell me about our family.

Which of your characters is most like you?
I'm not nearly as brave as any of my characters.

When you finish a book, who reads it first?
My editor, Reka Simonsen. I trust her judgment. I don't like to show it to anyone less qualified to tell me whether something works.

Are you a morning person or a night owl?
Morning. By noon, I am just a phantom of my morning self, and by evening, I turn into a sponge—all I can do is read, not write.

What's your idea of the best meal ever?
A Cuban guateque. It's a country feast on a farm. It comes with music, jokes, storytelling, and impromptu poetry recitals by weathered farmers with poetic souls.

Which do you like better: cats or dogs?
I love to walk, so definitely dogs. We always have at least one cat, but cats don't like to go places. Dogs are much more adventurous.

What do you value most in your friends?
Honesty and kindness.

Where do you go for peace and quiet?
A pecan grove behind our house at least twice a day, and the Sierra Nevada Mountains, at least twice a week. When I really need tranquility, I visit giant sequoia trees. Their size, age, and beauty help me replace anxieties with amazement.

What makes you laugh out loud?
Funny poems. The sillier, the better.

What's your favorite song?
I love the rhythms and melodies of old Cuban country music,

but my favorite lyrics are from a reggae song by Johnny Nash, "I Can See Clearly Now."

Who is your favorite fictional character?
That changes constantly. In other words, the one I am reading about at the moment.

What are you most afraid of?
Tidal waves, nightmares, and insomnia.

What time of year do you like best?
Spring.

What's your favorite TV show?
So You Think You Can Dance.

If you were stranded on a desert island, who would you want for company?
My husband.

If you could travel in time, where would you go?
My grandmother's childhood.

What's the best advice you have ever received about writing?
Don't worry about getting published. Just write for yourself.

What do you want readers to remember about your books?
Characters who never lose hope.

What would you do if you ever stopped writing?
Read.

What do you like best about yourself?
Hope.

What is your worst habit?
Self-criticism. Talking mean to myself. I can be very discouraging.

What do you consider to be your greatest accomplishment?
Finding the poetry in history.

Where in the world do you feel most at home?
Forests and libraries.

What do you wish you could do better?
Don't worry, be happy.

What would your readers be most surprised to learn about you?
My husband is a volunteer wilderness search and rescue dog trainer/handler. He and his dogs search for lost hikers in the Sierra Nevada Mountains. I hide in the forest during practice sessions. I am classified as a volunteer "victim."

After a devastating shipwreck, the first pirates
to sail the Caribbean suddenly find themselves
at the mercy of their teenage captive.

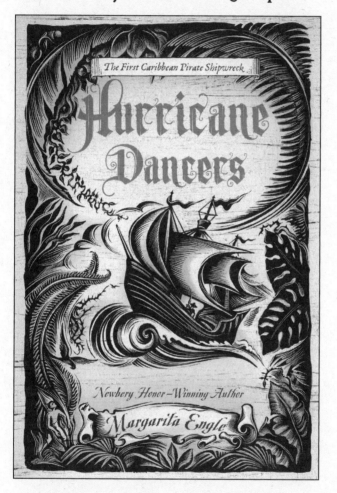

Keep reading for an excerpt from
Margarita Engle's next adventure

Hurricane Dancers

Quebrado

The sailors call me *el quebrado*,
"the broken one," a child of two
shattered worlds, half islander
and half outsider.

My mother was a *natural*, a "native"
of the island called *cu ba*, "Big Friend,"
home of my first few wild
hurricane seasons.

My father was a man of the sea,
a Spanish army deserter.
When my mother's people
found him on horseback,
starving in the forest,
they fed him, and taught him
how to live like a *natural*.

To become a peaceful Taíno,
he traded his soldier-name
for Gua Iro, "Land Man."
He and my mother

were happy together,
until a plague took the village,
and none were left
but my wandering father,
who roamed far away,
leaving me alone
with his copper-hued horse
in an unnatural village
of bat-winged spirits
and guava-eating ghosts.

Sailors call me a boy
of broken dreams,
but I think of myself
as a place—a strange place
dreamed by the sea,
belonging nowhere,
half floating island
and half
wandering wind.

Quebrado

I survived alone in the ghostly village,
with only my father's abandoned horse
to console me, until a moonlit night
when I was seized by rough seafarers,
wild men who beat me
and taught me how to sail,
and how to lose hope.

I was traded from ship to ship as a slave,
until I ended up in the service
of Bernardino de Talavera,
the pirate captain of this stolen vessel.

The pirate finds me useful
because I know two tongues,
my mother's flutelike Taíno,
and my father's drumlike Spanish.

Together, my two languages
sound like music.

Bernardino de Talavera

I once owned a vast land grant
with hundreds of *naturales*,
Indian slaves who perished
from toil, hunger, and plagues.
Crops withered, mines failed.
All my dreams of wealth vanished.

Soldiers soon gave chase,
trying to send me to debtors' prison,
so I captured this ship and seized
a valuable hostage, Alonso de Ojeda,
Governor of Venezuela,
an immense, jungled province
on the South American mainland,
where he is known
as the most ruthless
conqueror of tribes.

When I heard that Ojeda
had been wounded by a warrior's
frog-poisoned arrow,
I offered help, assuring the Governor

that my ship would gladly carry him
to any port with Spanish doctors.

I offered the illusion of mercy,
and Ojeda was desperate enough
to believe me.

Quebrado

The pirate demands a ransom,
but the hostage insists
he has nothing to give,
so while they argue,
I lean over the creaking ship's
splintered rail,
watching with wonder
as blue dolphins
leap and soar
like winged spirits.

My mother believed dolphins
can change their shape, turning
into men who come ashore
to sing and dance during storms.

If legless creatures
can be transformed,
maybe someday
I will change too.

Bernardino de Talavera

I catch the broken boy,
and it takes only a few quick blows
to convince Ojeda
of my strength.

When the prisoner sees my power
over a slave boy, he understands
that I would show even less mercy
to a grown man.

Knights who have lost
their guns and swords
are remarkably easy
to frighten.

Alonso de Ojeda

All my life, I have been triumphant.
On the isle of Hispaniola, I tricked
a chieftain by offering him a ride on my horse,
then trapping him in handcuffs.
I sent him away in the hold of a ship,
to be sold as a curiosity in Spain,
but a hurricane sank the vessel
while the chief was still shackled.
Expecting rebellion, I slaughtered
his queen and all her people,
to keep them from seeking revenge.

There were days when my sword
killed ten thousand.

Now, all those dead spirits haunt me,
and I am the one on a ship
in chains.

Alonso de Ojeda

Shackled to a rotting wall
in the ship's stinking hold,
I feel as helpless as a turtle
flipped on its back,
awaiting the cook's
probing knife.

I clench my fists
and struggle
to fight my way
out of the handcuffs,
while ghosts
gather around me,
watching
and waiting. . . .

Quebrado

The sky is alive with cloud dragons
and wind spirits.

When a sailor is almost swept overboard,
I wish that I had a gold ring in my ear,
like the one the pirate wears for luck.
His red shirt is meant to ward away
evil winds, and he ties a green cloth
around his head for protection.

The rest of us are dressed in rags,
except for the shackled hostage,
who wears armor and an amulet
with the painted face of a wistful saint.

I wonder if the saint looks so sad
because she knows how many people
Ojeda has killed.